The Journey to My Brave First Step

FROM
BROKEN
TO
Badass

Cindy Bell Gerhardt

FOUNDER OF BRAVE FIRST STEP

Nonprofit Organization for Victims of Domestic Violence

Published by
CINDY BELL GERHARDT
ATLANTA, GA
www.bravefirststep.org

Print ISBN: 978-0-578-83322-4

Edited by Carol Killman Rosenberg
Interior & Cover by Gary A. Rosenberg
Author Photos by Liz Moore, Amooré Photography
Sword, shield and crown tattoo, courtesy of
Alvin @ JP Alphonso Studios

Contents

Prologue

*S*peaking in front of an audience is like a drug to me—it administers a dose of pure adrenaline and makes my pulse race. I relish the butterflies I feel in my belly right before I step behind a podium. I've spoken at seminars, conventions, conferences, and churches. I've spoken with commissioners, governors, state and U.S. senators, members of Congress, and the U.S. Secretary of Education. On most of those occasions, I have felt quite confident and resolute.

Not this time.

It was the first day of our statewide PTA convention. A little more than 1,000 folks were funneling into the large ballroom where my thoughtfully designed playlist blared over the speakers. Most were just milling around, looking for the best seats for the opening session that afternoon. As I gazed out over the crowd, I could see chatty groups with matching school T-shirts and folks standing on chairs holding flashy posters that identified seating sections by county. I could hear shrieks of laughter and saw ladies who hadn't seen each other since the previous year exchange exuberant hugs. I watched as some people danced in the aisles, took selfies, or worked the room. Smiles abounded, and the energy level was high. These were my people, and this was most definitely my scene.

But, today, they would hear my truth. These members of my tribe would get a glimpse behind the curtain I'd kept tightly drawn. They would sit in deafening silence with eyes glued to the stage as I slowly peeled back my mask and allowed them to see who I really was—a patched-together quilt of brokenness, pain, anger, abuse, and fear sewn together with unbreakable threads of hope.

CHAPTER ONE

Gotta Know the Rules

I've always thought of myself as a "Southern belle flower child." These two mindsets may seem contrary, but I guess that's one of my gifts: I'm a paradox. Even though I was born in 1966, way too late to be old enough to attend Woodstock, the music and lyrics of that era, from artists like Joan Baez, The Beatles, Simon & Garfunkel, and The 5th Dimension resonated in my young, formative mind. I didn't just listen to John Denver—I *felt* John Denver. I was also influenced by country and gospel music. My parents often sang in the car, in the kitchen, around the piano, and especially in church. Music was part of our daily lives.

I received my first piano at age three. I'm sure there was a guitar somewhere among my early gifts, but it was the piano that called to me. Once I was tall enough, I'd climb up to sit next to my mom on the creaky bench of her antique upright, watching her fingers move across the keys with such speed and accuracy, much like I imagined a newspaper reporter would skillfully and hurriedly type a breaking story.

She taught me how to find harmonies when we'd sing trios with my dad. In our home, it was normal to belt out gospel music in the living room when company dropped by. Singing country songs with my daddy in the truck was the same. We'd turn up the volume and sing along with Hank Williams, Charley Pride, and George Jones. I loved pretending to be Olivia Newton-John or Tammy Wynette, and I had not a single doubt in my mind that I'd be a world-famous singer one day.

Elvis Presley was going to be my husband. Despite the age difference and the obvious geographical hurdle, my plan was to hone my talent, strategically place myself directly in his path, and then one day it would happen. *Bam!* He'd hear me sing, immediately become smitten, and love me forever. Not to spoil the suspense, but that plan failed epically. At the ripe age of ten, I experienced my very first, but most certainly not my last, heartbreak. My mama called to give me the news that my true love had died that warm August afternoon while I was staying with a great aunt in Opelika, Alabama. I remember wrapping the phone cord around my finger as I tried not to cry. I remember hanging up the phone, getting a less than comforting lecture from my aunt about why Elvis wasn't really a part of my life, and then lying on the bed sobbing real tears into an old, worn, once bright-red stuffed dog wedged between the pillows.

As the daughter of devout Christians and, more importantly, Southern Baptists, I grew up with a strict set of rules. Some came from the Holy Bible, and some from the invisible bible known as *The Do's and (mostly) Don'ts of the South*: Don't drink. Don't dance. Don't listen to "long-haired" music. Don't wear too much lipstick. Don't wear short-shorts. Don't wear a bikini. Don't use tampons. Don't date until age sixteen. Don't smoke. Don't like boys who smoke. Don't cuss. Don't get a tattoo. Don't like boys who have tattoos. Don't wear makeup until high school. Don't talk bad about others (*unless you are trying to get them help, bless their heart, in Jesus's name, Amen*). Don't tattle. Don't talk back. Don't talk in church. Don't get any grade below a B. Don't call boys. Don't stay out past 9 pm on weeknights and 10 pm on weekends. This last one even applied to the night of my (first) wedding rehearsal dinner. My dad had to seriously weigh out the decision to let my fiancé bring me home from the restaurant. After all, it was Friday night at 9:45 pm, and we might not come straight home.

Seriously.

The *Don'ts* far outweighed the *Do's*. But the *Do's* were always the best thing about being Southern. Do always have sweet tea in the fridge. Do offer food to everyone who visits. Do watch football games on Friday night, Saturday afternoon, Sunday after church, and Monday night. Do wear

FROM BROKEN TO BADASS

cowboy boots with anything you want. Do name the chickens, goats, and cows on the farm (but don't ask about them when they go missing). Do ride on the tailgate of the truck. Do dig your own worms when it's time to go fishing. Do learn to use a knife and gun. Do say *ma'am* and *sir*. Do say *Coke* to describe any fountain drink. Do bring a dish when someone invites you for dinner. Do call it dressing (don't ever call it stuffing).

I am only child. Did I mention that? Most folks are surprised when I tell them. I guess their expectation is that only children are spoiled rotten, get everything they ask for, and aren't used to elbowing their way through life. In our lower-middle-income home, we always had enough. We shopped at the local discount grocery store and Kmart. On Wednesdays, we ate at a real restaurant, and then went to church. Every other day, my mom had supper on the table when my dad pulled into the driveway. We went to my aunt's house twice a year to get brown paper bags filled with clothes that my older cousin had outgrown. Those days ran a close second to Christmas.

We went camping each summer, fishing on weekends, and visited family during the holidays. I spent most of my childhood outside, playing in the playhouse my daddy and my uncle built for me or pretending to be a cowboy or a rock star. I also spent a great deal of time on my grandfather's farm.

Chatting with the cows, chickens, and goats was always entertaining. However, at home, I was predominantly alone with a vivid imagination. There were the occasional visits from the neighbor's out-of-town granddaughter, the kid down the street who wasn't allowed in the yard, the friends who came home with me from church every blue moon, but for the most part, it was just me, a hairbrush that doubled as a microphone, and a small transistor radio.

If that was spoiled, then I'll take it.

CHAPTER TWO

Teenage Angst

As I moved into my teen years, I was a little behind the curve when it came to my girl-friends. They had feathered hair and boys who called, and they were allowed to go out on dates. They had slumber parties, went shopping at the mall, and knew all the latest styles. Don't get me wrong. I had style. It just wasn't "current."

Middle school was a struggle to fit in. I had a few close girlfriends, but I mostly related to the boys. My love of football, baseball, and anything outdoors made it easier for me to converse and be relaxed around them. Basically, I was the gal pal, the safe female boys could vent to, joke with, and ask for advice about anything. I was no pressure . . . no worries . . . not an option.

I'd seen Dorothy Hamill skate in the 1976 Olympics and fell in love with her wedge haircut. I thought it would be a great idea to try out. My uncle, the barber, always cut my hair, so it was rela-tively easy for him to attempt. The combination of short hair (during the Farrah Fawcett frenzy, mind you), no boyfriend, no makeup, and an awful bout with acne basically shoved me into the arms of bullies everywhere. I was a pudgy, zit-faced tomboy with elusive self-confidence just barely out of reach.

I vividly remember the day a rumor spread around school that I was gay. It started when a boy called me on the phone (finally!) to chat about his high-maintenance and often jealous girlfriend. Afterward, he told his girlfriend about the call and that I had pretty much agreed with all of his complaints about her. She started the rumor that I was gay to get back at me. I showed up at school the next day to find nasty words written on my locker, mean notes shoved into the door vents, and sneers from the girls. Even the guys walked by with their heads down, eyes averted. I was hassled in various ways for about three miserable months.

As I look back and recall the embarrassment and dread I felt each morning when it was time to catch the bus, I can't imagine what it's like for teens these days who face similar challenges. I wasn't gay, and the hurt caused by my classmates' prejudice and ignorance was dreadful. If the rumor had been true, it would've been unbearable. Kids can be cruel. Then they become adults.

As I was going through this, fortunately, two of my friends never wavered in their support of me. They were fellow band members, and we were compadres in our awkwardness and unpopularity. Today, I still have and value their friendship.

Band served as an extension of my musical life at home; it was my saving grace. I still played the piano, which will always be my first love, almost daily. But when I had a chance to join the band and the honor (although I didn't understand it that way then) of playing my aunt's clarinet from her high school days, I couldn't pass it up. Playing in a concert band introduced me to a genre of music we didn't listen to at home or in church. Classical, symphonic music with its movements, changes in tempo and volume, the solemn minor chords, and the uplifting major ones welcomed me into a new world. Band would become a constant for me throughout my school days and into college. I marched in parades, performed holiday concerts, and competed in solo and ensemble contests. I had not abandoned my dreams of becoming a famous singer, but the stage, the lights, the audience . . . I was just getting my first tastes.

I left my awkward years in middle school behind, stepping into high school with determination to find my tribe: The awkward, less popular, eat-lunch-on-the-breezeway kind of peeps. Those who watched *Star Trek* and *Star Wars*. Those who still liked dressing up for Halloween and took the Fine Arts electives. Those who didn't excel at sports, didn't get new cars for their sixteenth birthday, and didn't make the homecoming court. Sure, I had some friends who did a few of those things, but my inner circle, those I trusted to stick close by, found our own brand of cool. As a freshman, I finally had my first boyfriend. He dumped me after two whole weeks.

The next brave guy that year was a sophomore. He was in advanced classes, played D&D, drove his mom's station wagon, and had a quick wit that kept me laughing. He was also an incredible writer. We'd exchange notes in the hallways between classes. He seemed proud that I was his girl. I was proud that he didn't dump me right away. However, there came a time when he did, briefly. There was a much cuter girl who was allowed to date. Who could blame him, right? I was only fourteen, couldn't go anywhere on the weekends, and definitely couldn't be alone with him. We were "school daters" only. I could hold hands, pass notes, sit next to him on the band bus to away games (but only when my folks weren't chaperoning), and talk for thirty minutes on the phone at night. (The phone couldn't be tied up longer than that in case an adult wanted to talk to my parents.) Anyway, our breakup lasted only for about two weeks; he came back and seemed to be happy with the limited relationship I could offer.

We broke up for good his senior year. He taught me so much during those three years about life outside of my yard, about pushing myself toward excellence, and about being brutally honest with the one I'm with. Some of those lessons stuck. Today he is a professor at a U.S. Naval college and a published author. He did it right. My dad had been wrong about him. He was one of the good guys.

Throughout my middle and high school days, I continued to go to church regularly with my folks. Skipping wasn't an option, and for the most part, I really enjoyed going. I made some great friends there, ones who have stood the test of time. I remember how excited I was when I finally was able to join the youth choir. That was a huge deal, and it happened when I was in eighth grade. Back then, *youth* meant only high school, but our choir director at the time was pretty cool, and since there were only a couple of us who had an interest in joining, he decided to bring us in a little early.

I remember our first trip. We traveled to New Orleans and sang in a few churches along the way. I also recall how self-conscious I was about the dress we had to wear. It was a short-sleeved, knee-length dress, made from a polyester material that was slightly clingy. It hugged hips and other female parts. I had started to outgrow my pudginess, but I didn't feel comfortable in the dress. I looked around at the other girls and compared waistlines, leg length, and chest size. I felt, once again, like the ugly duckling in the group. I would make jokes about my shape just to get to the punchline before they could. That's a horrible habit I'm still trying to shake to this day. At age thirteen, I just knew my looks wouldn't get me where I wanted to go so music would have to be my ticket.

CHAPTER THREE

Just Tagging Along

When I turned fourteen and started high school, the church youth group had become another tribe for me. We weren't divided by age, grade, looks, or styles. I became friends with some older girls who, from my perspective, had it all together. One who I became particularly close with had the most beautiful dark hair and green eyes I'd ever seen. I'll call her Whitney. We had sleepovers. She introduced me to makeup, hot curlers, and romance novels. She taught me how to "lay out" and lather on the baby oil. She helped me discover a girl in the mirror who I kind of liked. I felt almost pretty.

By the time I turned fifteen, Whitney had gotten a car. She'd give me rides to church and she'd let me ride with her to hang out with the older kids at Pizza Hut afterward. She offered me a little freedom I hadn't had before. She even gave me my first bikini, which I hid from my parents, of course. Her folks and mine were best buddies. We'd visit their river house. They'd come to our house for dinner. Our parents sang together in a quartet, and on nights when they'd practice at the lead singer's house, we'd swim, shoot pool, or play tennis. I adored Whitney and always sought her approval. She was the big sister I'd always secretly desired, and I tried to be the best kid sister she could ever want.

When she started dating, our time together slowed a bit. I still wasn't allowed to date, but I definitely didn't begrudge her the chance. I can't remember the names or faces of the guys who were lucky enough to get a night out with her, but no one seemed to make the cut for more than a few months. While I'm sure that was frustrating for her, it was perfect for me. I could live vicariously through her retelling of romantic gestures, hilarious missteps, and first kisses. I just knew that, one day, we'd both find our Prince Charmings, buy houses next door to each other, and raise our babies to listen to Journey, Van Halen, and Foreigner.

Around that same time, our church hired a new youth pastor/choir director—I'll call him Sid. He looked like an Italian god. Tall, dark, handsome, and the size of the Terminator. We weren't sure what musical or pastoring skills he brought with him to the job, but everyone in the youth group was instantly mesmerized. He had charm, athleticism, and a charisma unmatched by any young or old man in the church. Or the community. Or, heck, even in the city. All the young men wanted to become Sid's friend, and all of the young ladies wanted to make him smile. I just wanted him to let me have a solo.

I had become one of the pianists for the youth whenever we performed on Sunday nights. As Sid began to familiarize himself with each of us, I became known as the tagalong. Never in the initially invited gang, someone would inevitably say, "Hey, what about Cindy?" It didn't really bother me all that much. Being popular wasn't in my deck of cards, but being the funny sidekick was a perfect role. I just kept plugging along, practicing my chords, rehearsing the lead solo . . . just in case. After all, I knew that one day the microphone would be mine.

Then it happened.

We were planning an Easter performance, an eclectic mix of songs about the Resurrection, and a few solo parts were being assigned. I held my breath. I looked down at the ground, hoping my eagerness didn't show. After a few names were called, none of them mine, Sid started the rehearsal. I wasn't devastated, but I was disappointed.

Once rehearsal was over, Sid approached the piano and asked me to hang back for a minute. He asked if I knew a certain song that had recently been made popular again on the contemporary Christian radio stations. When I said that I did, he asked if I could play it. I replied that I was sure I could learn it if I could just find the sheet music. And then it came. Those words, the look, that smile. "I'd like you to play and sing it if you are good with that."

I heard a roaring in my ears and felt every ounce of blood rush to my face. Honestly, I'm not really sure if what I said was remotely intelligible but what was screaming in my head was "YEEESSSSSSS!"

The night of the concert, in spite of my nausea, I actually made it through the song, hands and knees trembling uncontrollably. I looked out to see my mama beaming proudly and my dad clapping like I'd won a Grammy. It definitely wasn't great. It probably wasn't even good. But I felt like I'd taken the first giant step toward my dream, and that was enough. Over the next few months, Sid allowed me to join the elite group of girls who had frequent solos. I felt like I belonged. I felt like one of the pretty girls. I felt whole.

Coincidentally, over the next few months, romance was blossoming. Whitney and Sid seemed to be hugging longer, laughing together more often, and frequently sitting next to each other. He gave her rides in his sports car. He became roommates with her brother. He treated her like a princess. Whitney's dad was skeptical, but her mom was over the moon. Her daughter may have caught the eye of a pastor, who was also a semiprofessional football player on our city's league. An athlete *and* a man of God. What mother wouldn't be thrilled? They were doing everything the right way. They were taking it slow and respectfully. They were setting the example of how courting should be done.

CHAPTER FOUR

Happy Birthday to Me

I'm not sure which girl confided in me first, but she wasn't alone. On two separate occasions, over a period of a few months, two girls shared similar stories with me. Why they came to me, I'll never know. I guess I seemed safe. It was obvious neither of them knew about the other. Sid had made advances toward them.

In one case, the girl was alarmed. She told me that the director had made her feel uncomfortable, and she'd squirmed her way out of the situation. As for the other, she was torn between an interest in Sid and not wanting to hurt her friends by getting involved with him, especially Whitney. These girls were a close-knit group. They'd grown up together, went to school together, and had dated the same guys before (at different times, of course). But Sid was not like those guys. He had goals. He had direction. He was established—far above the high school boys they dealt with each day. He was handsome, way beyond cute. He made them feel mature, valued, and important.

The common thread in both stories was secrecy. No one could know. They weren't doing anything wrong. He didn't want to hurt anyone else. He couldn't fight his feelings any longer. He was trapped and unhappy. No one could make him feel the way they did. It was destiny.

They were right. I was safe. I didn't say a word. Not to Whitney, not to anyone. I think, deep inside, I was happy that the blossoming relationship that had taken my "big sister's" attention away from me would be over soon. I was sure that the girl who was torn up over her feelings for him would come forward and pledge her undying love and devotion, unable to keep her true feelings hidden. But nothing was ever said. I watched each week as everything seemed to operate within the status quo. Whitney and Sid, the happy couple, seemed happier; the other girl seemed quietly satisfied. I wouldn't dare ask, afraid to get sucked into a drama where I had no place. I guess I convinced myself that those two girls had misunderstood the situation, that Sid didn't really say those things, that he really wasn't *that* guy.

I couldn't have been more wrong.

It was Wednesday, November 10, my sixteenth birthday. Because it was Wednesday, church was not optional. I didn't mind a bit since I enjoyed hanging out with the other youth and was secretly hoping they'd have some cool party planned in the fellowship hall. And, it just so happened, they did.

Someone brought a cake, and my mom came back to the hall to see if I was enjoying the surprise. Sid asked my mom if I could join the rest of the youth at Pizza Hut, following church. I heard her explain that my dad was working the three to eleven shift and wouldn't be happy if I missed the 9 pm curfew. He assured her that I wouldn't be late and that he would even personally drive me there and home. Well, that absolutely set her mind at ease. And, honestly, it made my heart palpitate just a tad. I had never been in his car like the other girls had. How cool would it be to drive up to the Hut, on my birthday, letting all the kids see that I'm finally more than a tagalong or a last-minute thought?

That's something I never found out.

Once church was over, most everyone had left, and Sid announced that we'd have to stop by his place so he could change. No problem; it was on the way. I don't recall why Whitney wasn't around that evening, but nothing felt out of the ordinary to me. I thought I'd sit in the car, but he insisted that I come in and wait. I stayed on the couch. He offered me a tour of the place and took my hand to lead me down the hallway. What happened next is a blur of hands, lips, resistance, and compliance. I mentioned that I knew about the girls. That didn't help. He promised nothing "adult" would happen. He lied.

After grappling for what seemed to be an eternity with assurances that this wasn't crossing a line,

I was left on a wrinkled bed, covered in his sweat as he stormed out of the room, yelling for me to get dressed. I assumed I had won the struggle—that no matter his size or strength, my pleas and my squirms had worn him down to concession. I trembled and sat up, every nerve shaking and confused. I tried to walk across the room. I slowly made it to the doorway and found the light switch. I had no idea where my pants were and the room was pitch black. As I flipped the switch and turned toward the bed, the sight of blood hit me like a train. I hadn't made it out whole. I hadn't stopped it in time. I had just become a statistic.

Sid drove me home, barely speaking a word. He said he'd handle the explanation to those who had been waiting for us at Pizza Hut. When he dropped me off in the driveway, he leaned over and kissed my forehead and reminded me that we did nothing wrong. He said that he was unhappy and that no one could know.

Inside, my mom was waiting up at the kitchen table. My mama, the all-knowing, immediately knew something was wrong. She asked me to have a seat. She reached out for my hand as I began to cry. I told her everything. She told me she loved me, as tears fell down her face. She told me to change and take a hot bath. She asked for my clothes and my silence. While her biggest concern was my well-being, her second biggest concern was for my daddy's. If my father found out, he'd spend the rest of his life in prison. I would be okay; she would make sure of it. We'd find a way around this, and we'd end up just fine.

That couldn't have been farther from the truth.

In the weeks that followed, the fallout from that night could be felt in almost every family in our church. Oh, I didn't tell. Neither did my mom. Did I mention that Whitney's brother was Sid's roommate? Somehow he had deduced that Sid had fabricated the excuse for why we never made it to Pizza Hut (perhaps he'd found Sid's bedsheets in the washer, who knows), and things got crazy from there. Whitney's brother told his father, who told Whitney, who came together to our house to tell my father what they suspected and confront me. The last conversation I remember between my "big sister" and me consisted of her accusation that I had "allured" Sid (his story), my sharing what the other girls had confessed to me (which Whitney refused to believe), our tears and screams, and her one final question: "Did you have sex with him?" My answer? "I'm sorry."

After the scandal, Sid left the church. A year or so later, after I got my license and a car, so did I. I eventually found a nice little church that needed a fill-in piano player, which gave me my excuse. I couldn't bear the unspoken judgment. Now, don't get me wrong. There were some good folks who never shunned any of us. They loved us and accepted that this was just a terrible mistake and no one was really to blame because no one really did anything wrong. Since no one could prove that anything evil had happened and no one wanted to discuss it, we should all just put it behind us. It was all a misunderstanding, and we should just rejoice that no one got hurt or went to jail.

After all, God is good. All the time.

For years, I carried around silent guilt. Immediately following the incident, I was asked questions such as "What were you wearing?" and "Why didn't you run away or call the police?" They weren't really posed out of concern; they felt more like accusations, like I was responsible for allowing this to happen and that my behavior before and after may have indicated fault on my part. Back in those days, no didn't mean no. It meant that you just needed coaxing. I spent years digging through my memory and trying to recall what I could've done differently to spare myself this shame and disgusting milestone. My first experience wasn't one of gentleness and discovery; it was brutal. No young girl asks for that. Sweet 16 and ruined.

It would be some years before justice would be served, and I'd find a sense of closure. I was approached one day while on my job by a detective from a city a few states away who had a few questions about an incident in my past. Someone who had attended our church back in the day happened to be watching a news report while visiting that city. The report stated that a local high school football coach had been suspected of inappropriate acts with some female students. The footage showed the coach, handcuffed, being led to a police car. They recognized him immediately. They made a phone call. My name was offered as a possible previous victim. My testimony was taken by the state's DA, and on the day of the hearing, I was able to face him for the first time in eight years. By this time, I was a married woman and a mother of two. He was an older, well-respected member of his community. All that changed for him on our day in court.

The look on his face when he saw me in the courtroom confirmed two things for me: One, that he didn't recognize my new name as it appeared on the witness list. And, two, that I didn't imagine the events of that night, that he knew he had done something wrong, and that I was not the one to blame. He made a plea agreement that day, never allowing one victim to give testimony. His sentence did not match the crimes, but at least now he could no longer cover up his past.

The one regret that has haunted me to this very day is that I didn't speak up loudly. I allowed doubt and shame to silence me, and because of my silence, this man went on to rob other young ladies of their childhood. Sure, I know it's not truly my fault, but meeting the other victims and hearing their eerily similar stories broke my heart. They didn't blame me, nor did their parents. I hugged the girl who had the courage to speak up. I told her that she had prevented others from losing their innocence. I thanked her for being strong when I was weak. I hope that wherever these girls are today, their lives are rich with love and joy. They deserve that and so much more.

We all do.

CHAPTER FIVE

Give My Regards to Broadway

So, I'll give you a moment to catch your breath. That's a lot to take in when you're hearing it for the first time. I've left out the yucky details, but they aren't what is the most important. We'll get to that soon enough. Remember, all of this took place at church, which was separate from the rest of my life. At my high school, I was still the Cindy everyone knew: quirky and funny. Band was still a thing, and I was halfway through my junior year. I wasn't seeing anyone. I had just reached the age where I could finally date, but dating was the last thing I wanted to do.

Then came Christmas and a visit to a different church. My mom had been invited to play the piano at a Pentecostal church. Their regular pianist was on holiday. This was the first time I'd seen drums, guitars, and a baby grand piano on the pulpit platform in a church. There was a big screen with the words to the choruses over the choir loft. There was even a sound booth. I knew Jesus was everywhere, but it looked like he had much more fun here! So did I.

I watched the musicians exit the stage as the sermon was about to begin. They walked along the wall toward the back of the church, passing right by us as they headed to the sound booth. I remember blushing a little as the drummer gave me a smile and a nod. That night, after the evening worship service, they followed the same path toward the booth. This time, I sought out the drummer's gaze and was rewarded with a slight wink. That wink started a series of intentional encounters, including a New Year's Eve party, which resulted in a kiss and my second official boyfriend. I'll call him John.

Things moved along, slowly. My dad still wouldn't let me go anywhere alone with him unless John asked, and my dad didn't make asking an easy thing to do. Let's just say John and I spent many nights on the living room couch, listening to albums on the console record player. He listened to bands I'd never been allowed to before—Led Zeppelin, Black Sabbath, Judas Priest, and Rush. He knew every drum lick, cymbal crash, and bass drum hit. He was the most talented musician I'd ever met, having made his first album at age ten. Ours was a match made in stardom heaven.

Like most couples who attend different high schools, we were off and on a bit. I broke up with him at the beginning of my senior year, thinking that I needed to keep my options open. He came to my graduation with roses. I didn't appreciate the gesture like I should have. I was distracted by family and friends; he was hurt. It wasn't until my first year of college that I sought John out, hat in hand, to see if he'd give me another chance. By that time, he and the other musicians in the church had formed a pretty solid band that played around the area at local churches and revivals. He let me back in, and so did they. You're gonna get excited when you find out how that turned out. . . .

But, first, let's get through the end of high school. I had joined the chorus my senior year and had become drum major in the marching band. I played keyboard in the jazz band. I surrounded myself with musical opportunities wherever I could find them. I competed in local talent shows and the Junior Miss pageant, performed at church events, and even made a little money singing for weddings. I applied for a music scholarship to the local university but received a merit scholarship to the junior college. I played the piano at my graduation.

When I entered college, I decided to major in voice and minor in piano, drama, and dance. After all, I was a Fine Arts junkie who dreamed of being on Broadway in musicals and plays, which would eventually lead to a solo career and megastardom. I auditioned for and made the collegiate chorale. We had semester recitals, music theory, plays, and musical theater. I loved every single moment. When we weren't in private lessons or classes, we were gathered around the grand piano in the recital hall, playing and singing top 40 hits, choreographing modern dance moves, and secretly trying to outdo each other. We pushed each other to be better, and the unspoken competition was palpable. Some of those folks ended up in Nashville, some became music producers, and others ended up on Broadway. I ended up in the drive-thru at McDonalds.

The path to fast food was actually an easier one than you'd expect. You see, most afternoons, the chorale had rehearsals to prepare for the biggest trip they'd taken in years. We were going to New York City to perform at the St. Michael's Cathedral—oh, and maybe catch a showing of *Cats*. You know, no big deal. At that point, I had reunited with John and had begun playing with his band. One Friday night we had a gig at a revival in a city a few hours away. Knowing I would not be able to attend rehearsal, I asked someone to let my director know my predicament and that I'd make up for any lost time the following week. That Monday, I was met with a note on a department bulletin board that instructed me to see the director. It wasn't a pretty meeting. I had lost my spot on the trip. I begged. I pleaded. I cried. I bargained. I lost.

Let's just say that decisions made out of anger can alter your life's trajectory in a split second. I just knew that I had lost my one chance at the big time. I had envisioned myself in the Big Apple, walking the sidewalks, meeting directors and musicians, standing out in the crowd, and catching someone's ear. If I couldn't go the New York, I'd quit it all. I ran, crying, to the registrar's office and dropped every class. Even as she warned me that once she'd pressed the enter button, I'd lose my credits and my scholarship, I told her it didn't matter anyway. I left campus that day, drove to the beach, and walked along the shore.

How would I tell my parents? What in the world was I going to do now? There were dozens of questions running through my uncertain mind, but there was one thing I knew for sure. One more director had ruined my plans.

CHAPTER SIX

One More Try

$\mathcal{M}$eanwhile, the church band was gaining a little notoriety. The piano player and bass player had become a couple. The lead singer and bass player were brothers. John and I were still dating. We were quite the quintet. We played in church each Sunday and at the occasional venue on Saturday nights. One day, a guest at the church asked if we'd be willing to travel to Nashville and record a demo tape with a popular contemporary Christian label. Obviously, we were thrilled. To sweeten the deal, they worked out the chance for us to appear on the Grand Ole Opry. THE GRAND OLE OPRY. I remember the butterflies, the long day and night in the studio laying down tracks, the phone call I made to my folks after we left the stage, seeing country music legends Roy Acuff and Connie Smith, touring the Ryman Auditorium the following day, and being asked to sing on that stage. The experience was surreal and is a memory I won't ever forget. It was my first glimpse at the dream I'd wanted my whole young life, and as life would have it, it was my last one, too.

Circumstances with the band and our benefactors changed pretty rapidly. The demo was completed but never published. The other couple married and began their new life. The lead singer found other work. John and I were married in a fairy-tale wedding with a limo and a horse-drawn carriage. We had a sweet baby girl. Neither one of us was ready for such a commitment, but we did the best we could with much-needed help from our parents. Our daughter was raised by all of us.

Music was still an integral part of our lives. We joined a different church. He played. I sang. We even started singing together. We became the adorable couple who set the example of how it should be done for other youth. We bought a house. We entertained guests. On the outside, we looked like the perfect couple. Behind the scenes, we were drifting apart. We handled the pressures of adulthood differently. He played music with his friends, and I discovered night clubs. We were free from the rules that had bound us as teenagers, and that newfound freedom came with a cost. It cost us our marriage. In three short years, we parted.

Once we separated, my daughter and I moved back in with my folks. Not exactly the best move, but necessary. It was difficult, if not impossible, to go from being a young adult with unlimited freedom forced back under the rules of my youth. A curfew? A bedtime? Permission to go somewhere after work? My folks were trying to teach me to be a responsible parent, while I wanted to hold on to my short-lived independence. I had graduated at seventeen, married at nineteen, and became a mother at twenty-one. The chain had wrapped itself around my ankle again sooner than I had expected. There was much more of life for me to still experience. I felt like I was being punished. I felt like the universe hated me. I felt like a failure and that no matter what I did, I was a disappointment. This was as good as my life would ever get. A divorced, single mom who worked in a fast food restaurant. I had become a cliché.

Fortunately for all of us, we weren't there long. I had met a young Navy guy one Sunday during Rum & Reggae, a live concert, at a bar on the beach. Let's call him Luke. Luke seemed too good to be true. He was tall, rugged, and loved kids. He was stationed at the local base, and my daughter and I would visit him often. My folks weren't thrilled. It was too soon, he was too Hispanic, and my baby girl was too young and would be confused. None of that mattered to me. I wanted out of the house, and Luke seemed to want me just as I was, baggage and all. He was a romantic. He was a Texan. He was a bull rider. He was larger than life. And he was just a kid. We found an apartment, had a sweet ceremony on the beach at sunset, and started a new life. He separated from the Navy and began a series of manual labor jobs. He was skilled at framing, flooring, and restoration. He was eventually hired at the manufacturing plant from where my father had retired. Good benefits and shift work.

I got pregnant immediately. Luke's grandparents came down to visit. While he spent time with his grandfather outside, I was in the kitchen learning the secrets of authentic Hispanic cooking from his *abuela*, his grandmother. She was the kindest and most patient woman I had ever met, second only to my mother. I learned how to prepare homemade tortillas, menudo, chorizo, and migas. When we visited their home in Texas, I followed the tradition of the men eating first, being served by their wives, with our turn to eat coming after the men had retired to the patio for cigars and beer. I loved being a part of such a strong family-based culture. His mother, aunts, uncles, and cousins embraced our diverse family. For the most part, I was welcomed with open arms. Being the first gringa to join their family was intimidating, but I managed to smile my way through it.

Eventually, over the next couple of years, Luke and I would have two boys. I'd try to continue the traditions that were prevalent in his family while including a few of my own. My parents came around to acceptance and loved our children without hesitation. We found a church nearby and started attending regularly. I started singing in the choir. We hired babysitters and went out dancing once in a while. Everything seemed to be going in the right direction.

Then it took a wrong turn.

CHAPTER SEVEN

Hit Me with Your Best Shot

The first time it happened, I was completely blindsided. We had gone to a good friend's birthday party. She and her husband both worked with me, and we'd begun hanging out as couples. I was super pregnant with our first son, so I was the designated driver. We'd been there for a few hours when my friend's husband quietly approached me and asked if he could speak to me in private. Apparently, my inebriated husband had made inappropriate advances toward the birthday girl, and she was quite shaken up. He asked me to please take my husband and leave.

After a few failed attempts, I finally got Luke to the car, which he insisted on driving. He was in the driver's seat and would not budge. As I leaned down and attempted to take the keys from the ignition, he backhanded me onto the ground. The look in his eyes when he realized what he had done was not one of remorse. It was one of defiance. I was stunned. I couldn't wrap my head around what had just happened. When I was able to get up off the ground, I went inside to ask for help. I just wanted Luke to let me drive us home. I was terrified that he'd get us in a wreck, and I could possibly lose the baby. Honestly, I can't tell you what finally convinced him to move to the passenger seat and allow me to drive, but he slept all the way home. I couldn't stop my hands from trembling on the wheel.

I have to be honest and say that I wanted things to work out. I wanted to forget that he had tried to be with another woman. I wanted to believe that Luke wasn't a man who would cheat or, even worse, a man who would hit me. After the birth of our first son, the situation escalated. I'm not sure if it was because I had gained so much weight while pregnant or his frustration that he was now tied down and committed. We no longer went out. Well, at least *I* didn't. I tried not to provoke him and conceded all arguments to keep the peace. It didn't take much to uncover the anger. Fixing the wrong thing for dinner, not packing his lunch correctly, talking too long to a male friend, and wearing too much makeup or clothes that showed too much neckline—any of these things could start the fight.

I was miserable and couldn't figure out what to do. I didn't want to tell anyone, especially my folks. It had taken too long to get them to accept Luke and my new family. There was no way I would admit that I had made a devastating mistake. When our first son was three months old, I found out I was pregnant again. This plunged me into a depression. I was so angry that I was stuck here. I hated being trapped. Even worse, I kept asking myself who in their right mind would want a twenty-five-year-old, twice divorced mother of three? I had completely become unrecognizable to myself. I stopped going to church. Stopped singing. Stopped playing the piano. Stopped dreaming.

Our youngest was born on New Year's Day. The first time I held him while we were alone in the room with no one else there, I just stared at him, crying. I kept thinking that my only hope of happiness rested with my babies. My only path to salvation would be to focus on them. To be the best mom I could be. Follow the example my mom had set for me. Find a way to make things better. That worked for about a year.

During that year, I had begun to take martial arts classes. I had met the instructor while I was still attending church. His studio was not far from my home. I did not tell Luke that I was taking self-defense classes. I kinda lied. I told him I was going to aerobics (basically the same thing, right?). I told him I wanted to get my pre-baby shape back. He was all about that idea. I hid my uniform in the trunk of my car. I was afraid that if he found out I was taking a class that included men, he'd not handle it well. I took classes for a few months before the cat jumped right out of the bag.

I had asked permission to attend an "aerobics" competition about an hour away, but as usual, Luke insisted on driving me. As we pulled into the parking lot of the civic center, he noticed the uniforms of the contestants walking in. I gingerly pulled out my duffle bag and smiled sheepishly. "Surprise!" I said. "I wanted to make you proud that I could do something on my own." I was shocked when Luke actually nodded and seemed eager to see if I had learned anything. That day, I came home with two trophies and a huge shot of confidence. I'm not sure what he was thinking, but I had just seen the light at the end of the tunnel.

During the next year, I continued to train often. I became a star student. I couldn't afford the tuition, but the instructor allowed me to clean the studio twice a week as payment. I had lost my job after the last baby was born. Luke had attempted to entice a coworker of mine into bed, and I reacted by threatening to hurt her. Needless to say, I was fired—another example of making a snap decision out of anger. So, I started cleaning houses to make a living. It allowed me to have a flexible schedule to work around daycare and school. Even though it wasn't the type of job I bragged about, I took pride in my work and met some incredible people who became very important to me.

One of those was an old acquaintance I had met during my fast food days, Ken. He had worked as a technician at the automotive repair shop next to our restaurant. He and the other mechanics had come over daily for breakfast or lunch. They took care of our cars, and we snuck them extra food. They were always sweet and never inappropriate. That's what I remember most about those guys, and this one in particular. One day I ran into Ken at a Chinese restaurant next to the dojo. I was the restaurant owner's housekeeper and was stopping in to get my weekly pay. When he saw me, we chatted and he asked why I was there. When I explained my current occupation, he asked if I had room for one more home in my schedule. I needed the money. He needed someone to do laundry for him and his two kids. I agreed.

As I began to make my weekly visits to Ken's home, I noticed signs of a mature, loving single father. He baked a homemade cake for his daughter's birthday. He had their pictures and report cards on the fridge. He was raising his children in what seemed to be a normal home. I also noticed that he had guitars in his music room. That he looked remarkably like Kurt Russell. That he owned a motorcycle. That he kept forgetting to leave a check so I'd have to go to the shop for payment. This gave us time to chat often, to grab the occasional lunch, and to get to know each other a little better. I'd babysit for Ken's kids every now and again, and our kids slowly became friends. He'd ask about my work; I'd ask about his. He'd ask about my husband; I'd lie and say everything was perfect. After all, what good would it do to tell the truth?

CHAPTER EIGHT

Independence Day

*J*t was right before Christmas. My youngest baby was about to turn three. The middle one was four and the oldest was seven. I had continued my martial arts training and had achieved the rank of first-degree black belt. My twisted marriage with Luke had its ups and downs, mostly downs. When things were good, it was easy to pretend the bad never happened. When things were bad, I couldn't see any hope.

The car was having issues so we had taken it to have it checked over. While we were waiting, Ken asked if we had plans for New Year's Eve. My reply was that we couldn't because we were having a birthday party the next afternoon for the youngest. To the contrary, Luke's reply was that he had tickets to a big bash at the local country bar where he often worked as a bouncer. He had begun to work security at strip clubs, as well. Times were tough, and, as he often pointed out, we needed the money. So, with regard to New Year's, it became apparent that while I had no plans, Luke had plenty. Ken said that if I felt up to it, I was welcome to bring the kids over and celebrate with him and his kids. Luke thought that was a great idea. I thought something didn't feel right about his response.

The night of New Year's Eve, as I tucked my boys into bunkbeds that were not theirs, I heard the house phone ring. After Ken answered, he nodded and grimly glanced at me. I felt something catch in my throat. When he hung up the phone, his eyes looked sad and full of pity. He told me that it was Luke who had called and asked him if it was okay for the kids and me to spend the night at his home. You see, Luke was bringing someone to our home and he needed privacy. I guess I wasn't supposed to learn the real reason for the request, but to Ken's credit, he said he couldn't lie despite the "guy code." He apologized and assured me that we were welcome to stay until morning. The boys could continue to sleep and once the New Year clock had run down, he'd give me the bed and he'd sleep on the couch. He played his guitar for me, and I wanted to sing along but couldn't. That was the longest night of my life.

The next day, we all ate breakfast and then the kids and I made our way home. Ken had called ahead to "make sure the coast was clear." I felt sick to my stomach. I looked at my boys in their car seats and wondered how I had chosen this life for them. I couldn't confront my husband out of fear for myself and our friend. I would just have to tuck it down deep and pack it firmly next to all of the other hurts and disappointments buried there. I'd become quite skilled at living behind a mask.

It took four days before Luke asked me the question that I can only assume was burning a hole in him, like my truth was in me. He waited until the boys were playing in the other room, he brushed back my bangs gently, and asked if I had enjoyed myself on New Year's Eve. I answered that it was nice: the meal was delicious and the kids had fun but sleeping there was awkward. And then I saw it. That look I had grown to dread. His stare went flat, and he sounded like he was snarling when he pointedly asked if I had kissed Ken at midnight.

At that moment, I don't know why I did it. Maybe it was because of the anger and hypocrisy I felt at his accusation. Maybe it was because deep down I had wanted to have that kiss. Maybe it was because I wanted to make him jealous for a change, to make him feel that he needed to hold on to me, instead of my always feeling dread each time he left to go out. Whatever the reason, I felt my lips form a sly grin and I simply said, "Of course." I couldn't believe the lie had come so easily out of my mouth, but I couldn't take it back. What happened next was like a freight train roaring out of a station.

As if we'd danced this same dance a hundred times, we assumed the well-rehearsed positions. He towered over me while I crouched down as low as I could get. I felt the pain in my back as his fist came down. I began to whimper, and he called me a few choice names as he started to walk out of the bedroom. Hearing those names and feeling the sanctimoniousness of his accusation flipped some kind of switch in my head. I found the first thing my hand could grab, his steel-toed boot, and flung it toward the door, hitting the frame and then his shoulder. The look in his eyes was one of shock and disorientation. He stood frozen for a moment, trying to process what was happening. This bought me a few seconds to stand to my feet. There was no going back now.

The years of locking myself in the laundry room, of locking the front door to keep him out, of being left in places where I had to find my way home, of hiding bruises, of not visiting my parents until all visible signs were gone, of dreading the sound of a beer can opening, of cowering like a beaten down dog . . . all those images gave me the courage to stand to my feet and decide that today, January 4, would be my Independence Day. Win or lose, I was *never* going to get hit kneeling down again. I took each blow and answered it with one of my own. I felt no pain as our fists connected with body parts. I didn't see when the boys quietly locked themselves in their room. I didn't panic when his hands wrapped around my throat. I didn't think about what to do next, I just let my training and instinct take over.

At some point, once Luke realized I wasn't going to back down, he just decided to walk out. I had a moment of panic, like I always did when he left. But this time the panic wasn't because of what would happen if he returned. This time it was the realization that he may not come back. I pushed that absurd feeling aside momentarily and did the only thing I knew to do. I called Ken. I asked if we could come stay there for just a few hours. I felt safe there. The kids felt comfortable there. It would buy me some time to figure things out. We packed up a few things in garbage bags and sped away.

Garbage bags.

Years later, when I would hear about foster kids and how they moved from place to place, the visual of those garbage bags would bring these memories pouring back like a flood. It would be one of the threads that connected my story to theirs. Leaving a home, regardless how much pain it contains, is a heavy page to turn.

CHAPTER NINE

Go Your Own Way

*O*nce settled in his house, Ken suggested that I call the police to have a report of the incident. When they came, the officers politely reminded me that this wasn't my first call. They also informed me that since I had exhausted the number of calls that can result in no action taken, they were going to need to take one of us into custody. Him or me. I chose him. They also suggested that I seek medical attention immediately. I didn't realize the extent of the injuries I had sustained due to the adrenaline and relief.

I left the kids with Ken while I went to the hospital. I knew they would be in good hands. The ER was packed, of course. The humiliation I felt sitting in the waiting room and fearing that someone I knew would see me in this condition was overwhelming. When they finally called my name and escorted me to the room, they asked to take pictures to document the injuries. After suffering this additional indignity, the doctor finally came in.

I was anticipating a look of pity, like the one

I had seen on the nurses as I disrobed and posed for the camera. But what I saw was frustration and irritation. He reviewed my chart and acknowledged that this wasn't my first visit to this ER. He asked if I had pressed charges this time. I said yes. He asked if I was going to return to him, like I apparently always did. I said I didn't know. He shook his head and asked if I would at least consider being a good mother and letting someone else raise my kids. That statement floored me. Had I heard him correctly? Did he just accuse me of being a bad mother? Where was his compassion? Where was his sympathy for my plight?

In so many words, he explained himself. By staying and keeping the kids, I was teaching my daughter that it was okay to be abused, to be disrespected, and to be treated like trash. I was also teaching my sons how to become abusers. He was tired of the cyclical behaviors battered women continue to be trapped by. He reminded me that there was a possibility that one day I wouldn't make it into the ER. One day, I might not survive, and I would be leaving my children to be raised by an abuser. There it was. The one thing I knew that I wanted to do right and I had failed at it, miserably. Thanks to that doctor's harsh but heartfelt message that day, I finally made the decision to save myself and my children. His words changed my life, and I will be eternally grateful.

We never went back to Luke. I was determined to find a way to make it on my own. I would make the best decisions for my children. I would get back on the path to finding me again. The girl I had been was long gone. I had no self-esteem, I had no home, and I had no plan. Going back to my parents' house wasn't an option. With three kids in tow, I needed more than just one bedroom. Ken offered for us to stay indefinitely, and I reluctantly took him up on it. We found a way to fit five kids and two adults into a three-bedroom home. After a few months of acclimating to each other, our children began to form bonds. And, as luck would have it, so did we.

Over the next twenty-plus years, Ken and I would marry, raise our children, laugh, cry, fuss, and build a business and a life together. We would struggle through step-parenting. We would survive hurricanes and in-laws. We would argue over finances and ex-spouses. We would love each other and the kids unconditionally. He would be an example to my sons of how good men act. He would show my daughter how a woman should be treated. He would teach me how to walk on my own and to become independent and strong. In the end, aside from my parents, Ken's influence on my life is unmatched, and I am forever grateful.

When I eventually stopped my housecleaning job to work at the elementary school where the kids attended, my life took a dramatic upswing. What started as a temporary part-time job as a receptionist eventually blossomed into a full-time administrative role with my very own office. The years I spent working at the school would shape the next part of my journey, and more important, the journeys of so many others. I'll definitely discuss more of this later. Make a note.

Eventually, due to school district budget cuts (a term we use way too often), I had to find a new career. I had spent a summer working in one of my husband's shops and thoroughly enjoyed it. By this time, he had received the opportunity to not only become the owner of the location where he worked, but also to expand by becoming a multi-shop owner. Things were really looking up for us. I learned the point-of-sale system, how to order parts, opening and closing procedures, and so on. I enjoyed the shop environment and the people I worked with.

Ken brought me into the world of automotive repair, teaching me the ins and outs of the industry. I worked in that shop for a few months, and then I began to help him with the other shops he had acquired. Altogether there were six in four different cities, and he had his hands full with personnel, advertising, inventory, etc. I learned as much as I could, as fast as I could. I enjoyed the fast pace, the diverse customer base, and the travel between shops. I became fiercely competitive with the other owners within our region, always wanting to be in the

top five each week. I spent time with other opera-
tors, learning their methods of success, and I pushed
our guys to be better. It wasn't long before I was
offered a chance to move into a larger role within
the company. There would be extensive travel, and I
would have influence in a greater number of stores.
I jumped at the chance, saying yes before even asking Ken. Not that asking was required, but looking
back, it would've been the respectful thing to do.
Hindsight, you know?

I spent a few years on the road, staying in hotels
from Florida to Texas. I enjoyed the travel and the
opportunity to meet such a wide variety of folks
along the way. I have never regretted the decision to
take that uncertain step up the ladder, only the way
of life I left behind: our home, which we had built on
my family's farm, the quiet mornings sipping coffee
from rocking chairs on our back porch, and working
side by side to build a business. For some reason, I
still felt a gap that those things could not fill. I felt
unfinished. I felt that I was meant for more.

It seemed that as our children grew up and flew
the nest, Ken and I found ourselves struggling to find
connection. Our lives and conversations had always
been intertwined with raising the kids and work.
When I came home from traveling, it took a few
days to get back into the groove. By the time we did,
it was time for me to leave again. Finally, one day, I
left and never went back. Ken and I remain close to

this day, speaking regularly about the kids, grand-kids, work, and life. He knows me like no other, being a close observer as I grew into the woman I am today. I owe him more than I can ever repay.

CHAPTER TEN

Turning Point

*W*ell, you'd think that we'd be near the end, right? After all, I'm no spring chicken anymore and you're pretty caught up on the events that impacted the first part of my life. However, in between those previous chapters was an unwritten story about how the world of child advocacy became a thread that wove a meaningful tapestry out of my life—a beautiful depiction of brokenness and uncertainty, evolving into self-confidence and purpose. This world that I was about to enter would not only set me on a course of discovery and meaning, but would introduce me to some of the most influential and remarkable warriors I have been honored to call my friends.

It was the summer before my eldest son started Big Boy School. I was still cleaning houses at the time. I had taken him for his kindergarten evaluation. Yes, I said, EVALUATION. I was a nervous wreck. What if he forgot his colors or any of the big words that I had taught him so he could impress the teacher on the first day of school? What if he overshared all our drama at home?! (If oversharing to strangers was a subject, he'd ace it . . . just saying.) We signed in and then he was gently escorted out of the media center by his teacher. I was left standing with this group of grinning, devious ladies who were plotting to see what horrible, nasty volunteer job they could sucker me into taking.

After a few quick introductions and explanations of how wonderful and fantastic the school's PTA was, they got straight to it. I would be perfectly suited to co-chair the fall carnival. "What an easy job," they said. "You'll have lots of help," they said. "The teachers just love helping out," they said. They lied.

Well, the carnival was actually a pretty fun gig, so I kept it for a few years. Then I moved into other roles, and finally, when my youngest was starting fifth grade, I made the leap to PTA president. Honestly, I did it because I had only one year left so if I screwed things up too bad, I'd be moving into middle school and who cared, right? Plus, I had the opportunity to be on closed-circuit television each Friday to hand out school spirit awards . . . the microphone, remember? Big deal for me. Huge.

A year later, I ended my term, "The Baby" moved into middle school, and I was outta there. Sorta. So, I may have gone back on the first day of school the following year just to help the newbies navigate the BooHoo Breakfast and the trauma of dropping off their little preciouses at the classroom door. And

I may have gone back that afternoon to help with the car line. And there's a strong chance I did that for the entire first week. And the second. And quite possibly the third.

By the end of the first month of school, the principal called me into her office with an offer. I'll never forget the way she said it: "Look, you've been here as a parent for, what, eight years now? And it's obvious you really love volunteering, even though your kids aren't here at this school. In fact, that may be why you love coming here so often. Anyway, why don't we do this? Why don't I put you on part time at the reception desk? You can greet everyone as they come in, answer the phones, handle checkouts, and all the volunteers. What do you say?"

After about two seconds of pretending to ponder and weigh the offer, I jumped up, hugged her around the neck, and said, "Hell, yes! Let's do this!" And do this, we did.

Like I mentioned earlier, after about two years in the part-time position, I was promoted to a full-time administrative staff role. I had my own office, handled budgets and student records, arranged field trips, and processed lunch applications. In my own office. This was a far cry from scrubbing tubs and toilets for the rich folks. I became colleagues with the other staff and faculty. I was even named Education Support Person of the Year for my county! I learned the inner workings of the education system from a different perspective other than peering over the front counter. I saw the harsh realities of budget shortfalls and unfunded mandates. I experienced the frenzy and stress of standardized testing.

I was also exposed to the realities that many of our students were facing each day of their lives. The lack of stable housing, which made it impossible to fill out a lunch application to qualify for free or reduced lunch status. Students were sent to my office if they had no money for breakfast or lunch to "borrow" funds, and it was my job to call their parents to inform them of their lunch debt and encourage them to complete one of the dozens of applications I had already sent home in the backpack. Single mothers were living on relative's couches or staying with a friend temporarily. None of those providing shelter wished for their household income to be disclosed, so the forms returned each day, blank.

My heart hurt for those kids who were dropped off by taxi in the mornings, wearing the same clothes they had on the previous day. Or those who were picked up by a last-minute, unknown addition to their "blue card," given permission by a parent who was working multiple jobs and just needed someone to grab their child before they took a bus to an empty home. Each year during my time there, I would bond with another student whose story was heartbreaking. *Foster care, shelters, incarcerated parents, drug abuse, domestic violence,* and *latch-key*—these were all terms frequently used when discussing our frustration and concern in helping these kids once they left the security and safety provided by the school walls.

One day, a young boy stopped by my office on the way to the cafeteria for breakfast. I assumed he was coming to borrow money again, but he had a big grin on his face. He presented me with two pieces of paper: one, a completed lunch application, and the other, a picture he had colored of himself and his siblings with a figure who resembled me standing in the middle of them. Everyone in the picture was holding hands. It was a gift from him and his siblings, and he was equally proud of both documents. One meant that he could eat every meal without embarrassment, and the other was meant to show gratitude to me for never giving up on them. When he left my office, after giving me the tightest hug, I stared at the picture and bawled like a baby. All the years I'd spent volunteering in those hallways, and I had missed the signs. I hadn't seen the crisis. I hadn't asked if there was a need. These were my neighborhood kids, and I had no idea the trauma they were experiencing right in front of my eyes.

That day was a significant turning point for me. I decided that somehow, some way, I would do better. I'd open my eyes wider. I'd speak up for those who didn't have a voice. I would use PTA the same way they'd used me . . . to get a job done and done well.

CHAPTER ELEVEN

Get Up, Stand Up

While still working at the school, I began my climb up the volunteer ladder. I moved into positions on the county council board and eventually the state level. During those years, as my kids were moving into high school and graduating, the focus became less on improving their educational experience and more on making things better for all children. I was introduced to and worked alongside a team of advocates who were living out the original mission of the association, which is to help every child reach their full potential, regardless of social or economic hurdles.

You see, back in 1897, PTA was established by two women who were troubled by the welfare of children working in mines and factories. Immunizations were only for the wealthy, and in some communities, children were often required to work to support their families. Healthy nutrition and an adequate education were not priorities in many areas of the country, and the infant mortality rate was much too high. Their call to action was met with thousands of other concerned citizens, and that was the start of what is considered today the largest and oldest child advocacy association.

Sure, some misinformed folks may still think of it as a clique of cookie baking, gossiping, middle-class, stay-at-home, white soccer moms. For most of us, our first glimpse into PTA was our mothers showing up at school to help with a field trip or a play. Once I volunteered my mom to help with a headlice check. She really appreciated me for that one. I remember listening to the song "Harper Valley P.T.A." and thinking about all of the other mothers who worked alongside mine and wondering if those lyrics applied to any of them. In our quiet little Southern town, it was likely. However, what I learned as I dug in a little deeper is that today's PTA is a powerhouse. It represents families of all dynamics, all religions, all nationalities, all socioeconomic statuses, and all backgrounds. And the honest truth is, once Publix opened up in the South, I never baked cookies again.

I will always remember the first time I attended a workshop on advocacy. Before this, I had been to local and statewide trainings on topics such as how to be a good membership chair or how to attract more volunteers. But, for some reason, I felt motivated to check out this class. I believe the description mentioned that we'd learn how to talk with decision-makers. To me, that would be a principal or a school board member. The presenter that day was a school district lobbyist in a county further south. She was petite, dressed in a sharp blazer and skirt, and when she spoke, she did so with a confidence and candor that held my complete attention. She talked about setting appointments with legislators, getting to know their aides, and following up with e-mails and phone calls. She made it sound like meeting with a senator was no different from chatting with your Sunday school teacher.

She spoke about bills that she had encouraged representatives to pass, which could help the students in her district have smaller class sizes. She shared tips on how to dress, how much paperwork to leave behind, and how to address them and introduce yourself. By the time her workshop ended, I had taken four pages of notes and was already imagining myself sitting across from my school board member, ready to discuss bus routes and crossing guards. I was absolutely hooked! This went way beyond gift-wrap fundraising and organizing the carnival. This was real stuff! This could really make a difference. *I* could really make a difference. It was with this enthusiasm, once I realized there was a problem with some of the at-risk students in my own school, that I decided to take action.

First, I honed my speaking skills. I've always had the gift of gab, but I needed to learn how to speak in public and motivate others the way the lobbyist had inspired me. It just so happened that PTA had a workshop for that. To this day, taking that class is still one of my fondest memories. The presenter came out in curlers and a bathrobe, setting the tone for a workshop filled with laughter, clever tips, and the realization that if you believe in something, sharing it is a piece of cake!

Next, I surrounded myself with the movers and shakers: the folks who had been involved for quite some time and had moved into key positions within their communities. I nestled up close to a few who mentored me, broadened my capacity for leadership, and made indelible marks on my life. I watched them become school board members, district directors, and leaders in other associations. They introduced me to decision-makers and superintendents. They put me in the same room with folks I had read about in the newspaper or had seen on the evening news. They treated me like I belonged, like one of them. And for the first time in what seemed like an eternity, I started to believe in myself again. I saw glimpses in the mirror of the confident young woman I had set out to be. These women believed in my potential, and as a result, I pushed full steam ahead.

The day I was installed as president of Florida PTA, I unveiled my plan. On a stage in front of hundreds, including my family, I shared the story of that young boy with no lunch money. I shared that eventually he and his siblings were broken up into separate foster homes. I shared that he ended up in the juvenile justice system and that I had no idea what had become of him. I choked up as I admitted that I didn't do enough. In my position at the time, I didn't know what to do. But now, as a leader of an advocacy association whose main mission is to provide hope to all children, I could see clearly. I asked that they join me in finding resources for families who are in crisis. That as a state, we start backpack programs for weekend meals in schools that do not have one. That we put together parent resource rooms for those looking for housing and temporary assistance, including food pantries and clothes closets. That we don't do like I did in my office each day . . . wait for someone else to find a way to help. That *we* become the answer.

For the two years of my term as president, I was overwhelmed with stories ranging from homes being built to foster care programs being inundated with suitcases filled with blankets, books, stuffed animals and underwear, called First Night bags, as well as basic necessities for those youth aging out. School lunch debts were being wiped out by community partners. Our members were advocating at the state level for juvenile justice reform. We started a grassroots coalition with other organizations whose mission to help underserved and at-risk students aligned with ours. We were making tangible, visible progress in helping children and families. I was so fortunate to meet volunteers all across the state who were being the hands and feet of these vital programs. I heard encouraging words, sweet compliments, and undeserved accolades. Then one day, I heard something that broke my heart.

CHAPTER TWELVE

Truth to Power

*O*ne evening, after hosting an educational summit on immigrant families and child trafficking, a young woman approached me with tears in her eyes. She was so glad that we had brought these topics to the attention of our members, and after a long, gripping hug, she looked me in the eye and said, "I'm so thankful for you and the other leaders. I wish so much that I could do what you do one day, but my life is such a mess. I could never be like you. You're so put together and well spoken. I'm not educated and refined like you and the others."

I stood there, feeling her misplaced admiration, and just shook my head. How do I explain to her that I wrote the book on messy lives? How do I tell her that any amount of education I received was from attending workshops and gleaned from the brilliant people I've surrounded myself with? How could she not see that I'm a glued together patchwork quilt of heartache and bad decisions? That night in my hotel room, I realized that I had one more story to share, a story that would not only challenge folks to do more for others but also demonstrate that each of them had within themselves a unique destiny. That's when I knew what my final speech to my tribe would reveal.

I'd share my real story. I'd tell them about my sixteenth birthday. I'd let them know about the abuse of my second husband. I'd show them that I wasn't put together. That I wasn't to be placed on a pedestal. That I understood when in a room full of hundreds of women, the likelihood of someone who had endured the same trauma as I had was overwhelming. I needed them to know that they weren't alone. That healing is possible. That I didn't make it through without the help of others, and now it was my chance to turn around and grab the hand of someone else who needed saving. My story could've ended in a hundred different scenarios, but because it ended the way it did, I felt a powerful urge to demonstrate to others that there is hope. There is another way to finish. There is a different path to take.

That brings us back to where you joined me on this journey, as I recalled the day I stood at the podium, full of trepidation and resolve. I told the group about my traumas, but I primarily focused on my heroes. I pointed out that the last young victim of the choir director had given me hope. I shared that the emergency room doctor had stopped the cycle of abuse and the martial arts instructor had shown me my strength. I asked them to reflect on the course of their lives and recognize how many heroes had quietly and unobtrusively changed their path. I also pointed out that, every day, children come into our lives who need us to be a hero to them—unobtrusively and quietly.

As I took my time to read each paragraph, trying not to rush but be deliberate in the delivery, I only dared to look up occasionally from my script and make eye contact with a few who already knew parts of the story. Their nods helped me find the strength to press on through the quiet stillness of the crowd. Once I had finished, I looked up at the gazing eyes staring into mine and offered a smile and slowly exhaled. The entire room seemed to mimic me as they let out a collective breath. Applause erupted, and even though it seemed that some were still processing, the faces staring back at me were smiling, either from what could have been appreciation that I had been so candid and forthcoming or maybe from relief that a weight had been lifted. Perhaps some realized that if I could tell my story without fear of condemnation and rejection, so could they. Many of them privately approached me throughout the day, some with wet lashes or red-tinged noses. They thanked me for sharing and came in for a hug. I didn't press, and most didn't offer, but I felt that maybe their stories were similar, if not worse.

Regardless, my heart was heavy as I held them close. I was more than willing to share their burdens if they were willing to open up. I knew that while I didn't have all the answers to recovery, I knew that it was possible. I hoped that I would have an opportunity to help when someone needed me, now that I had come out from behind the mask. That opportunity came sooner than I expected.

One Sunday afternoon, just a few months later, I was driving down the road headed to the local grocery store. There was only one other car on the road besides mine, and it was right in front of me. Without any warning, the driver slammed on brakes and a young woman jumped out of the passenger side. She hurriedly opened the back door and grabbed a young boy and his backpack. They rushed across the road, behind their car and in front of mine, and as she passed, we made eye contact. I could've sworn I saw her lips form the word, "Help." As she made her way to the sidewalk on the other side of the road, the driver of the vehicle swerved into the paved median and jumped out of the car to run after them.

He was a young guy, about average height and weight and appeared to be unarmed. Without hesitation, I pulled into the median behind him and started watching in my side-view mirror as he approached them. I didn't really have a plan. I did have a few forms of protection in the car with me, but using them would've been a last resort. While I'm more than capable of handling a variety of weapons, I never think of them as a first measure. (I know, that's a debate for another day.)

After a short screaming match, the young man conceded that they were not coming with him and returned to the car. He screeched the tires, made a U-turn, and drove by them one last time. I backed up my car so that my window was within earshot and asked if they wanted a ride. She nodded, and I jumped out and opened the doors for them. After they settled in, I drove them home. We introduced ourselves, and I made small talk to ease the tension as we made our way. I'm sure she was embarrassed and unsure. I didn't want to pry, but I definitely wanted to assure her that, whatever the situation, being in a safe place for both herself and her son was the most important priority. If they weren't safe at home, I'd find a place for them.

After taking them home, I gave her my phone number so she could reach me if she ever felt the situation called for an escape. I also assured her that I knew firsthand how this story goes, and that if she just wanted to talk, I was only a phone call away. I left them at their apartment, hoping that she'd follow through with my request, if not for her, then for her son. I hoped that my experience could help her avoid a similar story.

To this day, we still stay connected—not as much now as in the year that followed, but as often as we can. She moved and found a good job, and her son is adjusting well in his new school. I'm so proud of the progress she has made, and I hope she knows how much she and her son mean to me. Her story could've ended so differently, but she's strong and resilient, even more so than she realizes. My hope is that one day she can help another young mother who finds herself in crisis and that her son will grow up into a young man who understands how to treat those he loves.

Over the last couple of years, I've had other opportunities to help someone in an abusive situation. I don't think it's that I'm a magnet for the broken; I think it's more that I recognize the signs sooner than most would. If I hear voices that are elevated, I observe to see if the argument escalates. I recognize the flinch. I know all too well how fast you must react to an incoming strike.

It's not that I feel like Wonder Woman in search of women to save from bad decisions. It's that I feel more like Harriet Tubman, who escaped imprisonment and went back to help others. Harriet Tubman: the courageous woman who didn't just celebrate her freedom, but who jeopardized her well-being by daring to go back into the pit of hell to show others that freedom was indeed at their fingertips if they'd only be brave enough to choose it. That liberation was at the end of a long road that began with one bold step.

Don't get me wrong. I'm no Harriet. I wouldn't even begin to compare my works with her history-making endeavor to save countless lives. But what I do envision is something similar to what she created: a network across the world, connected to women and men who have known or may be a survivor of domestic violence.

Imagine, if you would, that a woman who lives in Bethlehem, Pennsylvania, decides to research her community to see if there are resources available for someone who wishes to change their life and find safety. If she finds that there are limited or no resources at all, then she commits to helping organize a path to security and well-being should someone near her need intercession. What if that woman had friends and family across the country who had also committed to be a part of the network? What if the chain spread from coast to coast? What if, no matter where someone reached out for help, there was a hand available to mentor, guide, encourage, and hold?

CHAPTER THIRTEEN

Straight, No Chaser

So, what's the point? Why share my story with strangers? Why spend months recalling both the seemingly insignificant and the pivotal moments in my life? Why revisit painful memories and open old wounds that could cause family and friends additional regret? It's simple, really. By speaking their truth, so many others have impacted my life. Honest, unfiltered, unbridled truth. I owe it to them to speak mine. They gave me the courage to give the world a glimpse of who I am. Here goes:

I have amazing, strong parents who have always loved me and whom I adore. I have three incredible children and two more I have had the honor of raising. Each of them have gifts and talents that make me proud each day, and I pray they create a life that brings them fulfillment. I would give my life for any of them. I have three beautiful grandchildren who call me Big Mama. They cause me such worry, yet bring me such joy. I relish each moment I have with them. I have family I am close to and family I rarely see. But my love for them is constant.

I have a tribe of friends I would walk through fire for, no questions asked. As an only child, never knowing the closeness siblings can have, I have to assume that this unconditional bond I feel for my group of chosen sisters and brothers comes just as close to blood. I never feel alone.

I have held a variety of jobs up until now, but I take great pride in my work ethic and my ability to adapt and learn new skills. I still have no idea what I want to be when I grow up. And I'm not really sure that I want to do that, either. Perhaps I'll open a pub, or a B&B, or a tattoo studio. Or maybe all three. Who knows? Maybe I'll end up on Broadway after all. Whatever I end up pursuing, wherever that may be, it will not be for the money. It will be because it makes me feel complete.

I still love music with a passion. I play the keyboard occasionally in the privacy of my office. I have attempted the local open-mic scene, but smoky bars aren't for me. These days my concerts take place in the car with my granddaughter, where we sing Disney songs at the top of our lungs. When she tells me that I sound just like Ariel, I realize that my dream has come true. To her, I am a rock star.

I love my volunteer life, which connects my passion for advocacy with the voices of others. Those whom I have battled alongside are also part of my family. I enjoy debate and making others smile, and I'm always intent on being the funniest person in the room. However, I do not want to be the smartest person there. I thrive on surrounding myself with those who can teach me to step out of my comfort zone and into new places that stretch my intellect and my being.

I don't back down from a fight. I won't tolerate bullying, and I can't abide self-centeredness. I hate racism in any form, and I believe that when the bible says, "Love your neighbor," it means every single person within our reach. If you have access to the internet, that means pretty much everyone on the planet. I don't believe that tolerance means disregard for wrongdoing. I just believe that all correction must come from love. If we don't take care of those who need help, then we aren't really demonstrating the greatest commandment, are we? This doesn't require *what-ifs* or *but-theys*. It just requires love. Simple.

I don't take compliments well, mostly because I feel uncomfortable believing them. I still self-deprecate on occasion, but I am honestly starting to love my body and my wrinkled face. I'd never spend a dime to change any of it. You get what you get. Sorry 'bout it.

I have tattoos—thirteen, to be exact. Each one has meaning and history. I started at the young age of forty and have gotten one for my birthday each year since. The one shown on the cover of this book—the sword, shield, and crown—represents this endeavor:

to fight for others, to protect them from harm, and to remind them of their royal birthright.

When I love, I hold nothing back. I'm all in. I have fallen in love a couple of times, and yet I'm on my own once again. I no longer believe in the fairy-tales promised within the pages of those ridiculous romance novels. I just hope for companionship and honesty and to be held by an embrace that brings warmth but also allows room for growth and spontaneity. (Don't squeeze too tight.)

I'm not one for merely observing life. I need to smell it, taste it, touch it, and scrape my knees up exploring it. I love the outdoors, football, and food. I want to hike mountain trails, kayak ice-cold rivers, and swim in tranquil lakes. I want to see every corner of this country and visit the iconic baseball stadiums. I want to lose my breath as I gaze up at the northern lights and squeal like a child when I make snow angels in the Rockies. I want to drink a beer in Boston, eat pizza in Chicago, and drink coffee from a camp stove in Wyoming.

I have made more mistakes than I have had successes. I have committed sins against my beliefs. I have hurt people, both accidentally and intentionally, with my actions and callous words. I have failed often to live up to my mother's perception of who I am. I have used people for my own self gain, and I have lost good friends because I took them for granted. I have missed out on opportunities because of fear. I lived my early adult years recklessly and without concern for my middle-aged self. I did not take care of my health for many years. There were times when I had little regard for my self-worth and frivolously gave my value away. It took years to become the woman I see in the mirror, the woman who some call a warrior.

I am alive, and from this moment forward, I don't want to waste a moment. I survived the unspeakable. I swam up from the depths of the murky waters and rose to the surface to breathe fresh air. I am not a victim. My past has no power over who I am today. I chose her. I chose freedom, and I have chosen to free others.

I know that I have a purpose. I know that you do, as well. Regardless of the past, our future is within our control. Each day we make decisions that impact not only our lives but also the lives of those around us. Each kind word we say, each person we let into traffic, each blessing we receive and pay forward, all these actions touch someone else, which in turn, starts a chain of events that can influence many. It is my hope that in some small way my story has made an impact on you. If you have hurts, let's talk about them. If you have made it through your hell, then let's work together to bring others out of theirs. Each day there are people who don't make it out, who feel alone, who feel no hope. Let's give them hope.

A Call to Action

So, I have a plan. This plan has lofty goals. First, I want the proceeds from this book to be the beginnings of a nonprofit that bridges the gap between places with abundant victim resources and communities with none. I want to find volunteers who are willing to be at the ready, who will offer, with no hesitation, a shoulder to lean on, a couch to sleep upon, or a ride to a shelter. I am not asking anyone to put themselves in harm's way or come out of pocket to aid someone in need. I am merely asking for the willingness to provide whatever you can, whenever you can, to whomever raises their voice and asks for freedom.

In this country each day, there are an average of twenty people per minute who are physically abused by an intimate partner. In a typical day, there are more than 20,000 phone calls placed to domestic violence hotlines nationwide.* For every case

* Source: National Coalition Against Domestic Violence (NCADV)
– National Statistics: https://ncadv.org/statistics

reported, hundreds go on silently. The statistics for mortality will astound you. Children who witness this type of violence are three times more likely to become abusers. However overwhelming this may seem, this is not a problem too big to fix. It is not a dirty secret to be swept under the rug. This is a reality in so many homes where kids are confused, hurting, and suffering. Often, the easiest action for a young mother is to stay in an abusive scenario, hoping things will get better, thinking she is making the best decision for her little ones by sacrificing her well-being. We all know that the hardest decision is to seek counseling or leave.

Let me be clear about a few things before you misunderstand me: I do realize that men are not the only abusers. I know that many young fathers are in the same situation with no ability to ask for help. Statistics show that one in nine men have experienced physical and emotional violence. Society and its fascination with machismo has placed such a stigma on a man who would "allow" a woman to abuse him that his cries for help are rarely audible. I'm not negating their plight. I'm merely speaking from my own experience as a mother. Help knows no gender, age, color, or social status. It's available to all.

I also recognize that therapy and counseling can be viable options for couples to consider before making the decision to end a relationship. Oftentimes, those who demonstrate the aggressive behavior have been the victims of those same types of offenses as children or youth. Everyone deserves a chance to receive help, make changes, and become a better version of themselves.

Next, abuse is not only physical. It can be verbal and emotional. While my experiences included all of the above, that does not mean our focus should be only on those who have visible marks and bruises. Some of these invisible scars can last for a lifetime. Abuse of another's affection, devotion, trust, and dependence is intolerable. Period.

Listen, I'm just one person. One brave, badass woman who has learned to not only stand up for herself but also for others. There are more of you out there. I feel you. I hear your heartbeat as I type these words. Together, and only together, can we form a network of warriors who will offer shelter, safety, and hope to a generation of future warriors who will raise their children to be compassionate, loving, strong, and resilient men and women. And when we are long gone, they'll remember that we not only found our way to freedom but that we also turned back, stretched forth our hand, and showed them the way to a more abundant life.

Will you help? Will you find within your comfort level the means to contribute either time or resources? Will you raise your hand to be at the ready? Will you share this story or yours when the time comes? Can I count you in the tribe of warriors who are ready to do battle on behalf of someone in need? You'd be amazed at how the smallest gesture, a phone call, an e-mail, or just a hug can make the difference in someone's decision to make a leap of faith. Your words may be the catalyst in helping stop a cycle of abuse and neglect.

Finally, if my story resonated with you, if you found any similar passages, if you have held on to a wound so deep that you never felt that healing was within your grasp, please reach out. If not to me, then to someone nearby. I'm always here. I can always make the time to listen. I will find a way to offer guidance. If I'm too far away, I'll find a warrior nearby, who has answered the call. We will not let you fall. We will not turn away. We will show you the path to freedom if you'll only take that brave first step.

I believe in you.

For More Information

For more information about **Brave First Step** or to find out how you can be part of this movement, please contact me at abravefirststep@gmail.com.

For more info, please visit www.bravefirststep.org.

At Brave First Step, our mission is to provide for the urgent needs of victims of domestic abuse, by connecting them with resources and sanctuary, as well as to work within communities to develop new or enhance existing programs already in place.

About the Author

Cindy Bell Gerhardt is a native of Florida and currently resides and works in Georgia. She has been a volunteer in many associations for over 25 years, including mission work abroad, homeless ministries locally as well as child and family advocacy nationwide.

She has raised a family of five children, which now includes three perfect grandchildren. Her work with non-profits began as a labor of love to stay involved and connected in the lives of her children, and has now blossomed into the desire to create safe and nurturing spaces for all children and families.

In the creation of a new project, Brave First Step, she hopes to use her life experiences to help other victims of sexual assault and domestic violence find the courage to find help and the resources to reach healing and recovery.

Made in the USA
Coppell, TX
03 February 2021